First Lesson Cajon

by Jordan Perlson

	Audio Contents		
1	Example 1	18	Example 47
2	Example 3	19	Example 49
3	Example 8	20	2nd Endings
4	Example 12	21	Dynamics
5	Example 14	22	Example 51
6	Example 18	23	Example 52
7	Example 19	24	Example 55
8	Example 24	25	Example 58
9	Example 26	26	Example 60
10	Example 28	27	Example 62
11	Example 31	28	Example 63
12	Example 32	29	Example 64
13	Example 35	30	Example 66
14	Example 39	31	Example 68
15	Example 41	32	Example 70
16	Example 43	33	Example 71
17	Example 45		

1 2 3 4 5 6 7 8 9 0

© 2012 BY MEL BAY PUBLICATIONS, INC., PACIFIC, MO 63069.
ALL RIGHTS RESERVED. INTERNATIONAL COPYRIGHT SECURED. B.M.I. MADE AND PRINTED IN U.S.A.
No part of this publication may be reproduced in whole or in part, or stored in a retrieval system, or transmitted in any form
or by any means, electronic, mechanical, photocopy, recording, or otherwise, without written permission of the publisher.

Visit us on the Web at www.melbay.com — E-mail us at email@melbay.com

Table of Contents

Introduction 3
History of the Cajon 4
Sitting at the Cajon 5
Striking the Cajon 6
Basic Rhythm Fundamentals 9
Time Signature 10
More About Counting 11
Counting Eighth Notes 12
How to Practice 13
Sixteenth Notes 16
Ties and Dots 18
Dots 19
Form, Repeat Signs 20
Pop and Rock Beats 21
2nd Endings 24
Dynamics 25
Ghost Notes 26
Brushes 27
Flams 29
Wrapping It Up! 31

Introduction

Welcome to Cajon First Lessons! This book is designed to give you a basic understanding of rhythm, getting a sound out of the cajon and finally, playing it in a pop/rock context.

Never played an instrument before? No problem! You will learn the basics of reading rhythm and how to apply that knowledge to playing music. By the end of this book, you'll be comfortable with notes, rests, dots, ties, repeats and all of the other ingredients that go into reading rhythm!

Getting the right sound out of the cajon can be a little intimidating but have no fear! The section on sitting on and striking the cajon are simple yet detailed. In addition, the audio CD will help greatly in fine tuning your personal sound on your instrument.

The cajon is an incredibly fun, versatile instrument used in many musical contexts. In this book you'll find examples preparing you for many of those contexts. Remember to take things slow and not to move forward until you are comfortable with the section you are working in. This isn't a competition…it's music!

History of the Cajon

The word "cajon" comes from the spanish word *caja*, which means box. African slaves were not allowed to bring their drums with them when they were forced to leave Africa for regions like Peru, but they would not let that stop them from making music. The earliest cajons were empty fish boxes, often with loose tops that when struck, would "slap" against the back of the box. As well, many boxes were held together with loose or cheap metal that rattled, creating a "snare" effect.

Other early cajons were dresser drawers in Cuba. Cuban musicians would salvage discarded furniture on the street and use the rectangular shape of the drawers to sit on and play.

The cajon eventually made its way to Spain where it became the predominant drum in Spanish Flamenco music, complimenting the acoustic guitars, singing, clapping and rhythmic dancing perfectly. Commonly, the Spanish style cajon has some kind of "snare" apparatus and the Peruvian cajon does not.

Cajon construction is fairly simple. Modern day drums have some kind of tightly wound metal string, much like a guitar string, running up the striking side of the drum.

This drum, for instance, literally has guitar strings strung up the striking side of the drum with guitar tuners at the bottom to allow the percussionist full adjustment of the string tension. This makes it possible for a large range of sounds.

*image used with permission, www.swanpercussion.com

Sitting at the Cajon

First thing's first. Sit down on your cajon with your legs to either side of the drum. Experiment with finding a comfortable way to sit at the cajon where your ankles are within a few inches of the drum and the palms of your hands can reach the center of the striking surface.

For most, reaching the center of the cajon means leaning forward. Make sure to *lean* and not *bend*! Slouching leads to poor posture which leads to back problems. We want to make sure we can play the cajon for the rest of our lives! No back injuries please!

Striking the Cajon

Fortunately for us cajon players, what goes for one hand also goes for the other. Apply the following instructions to each hand, one at a time. Start with your dominant hand. Once you feel comfortable with each sound with that hand, read back over the striking instructions for your non-dominant hand.

There are two notes, or tones, for playing the cajon.

Bass Tone

1) Open your hand so it is flat with your fingers comfortably spread.

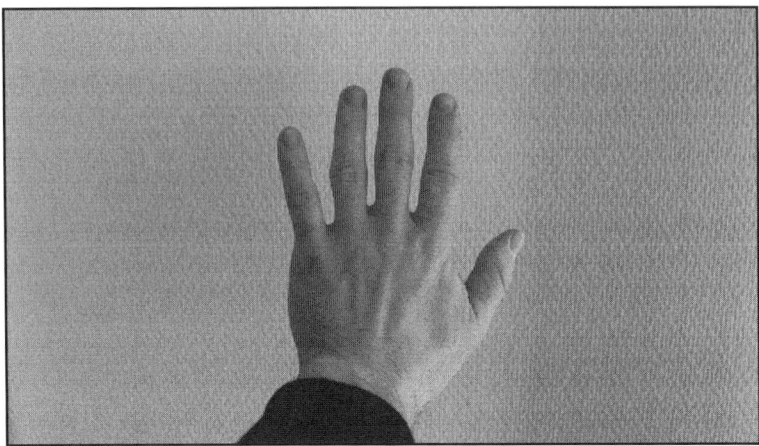

2) Straighten your fingers while keeping your fingers and palm relaxed.

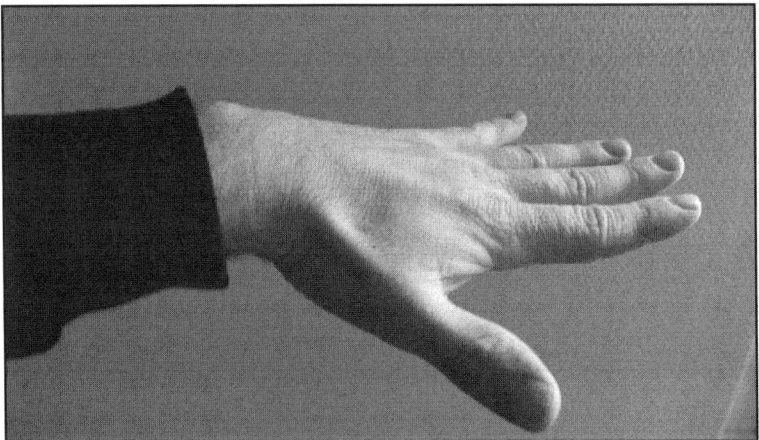

3) Place your arm so that it and your hand are parallel to the surface of the drum.

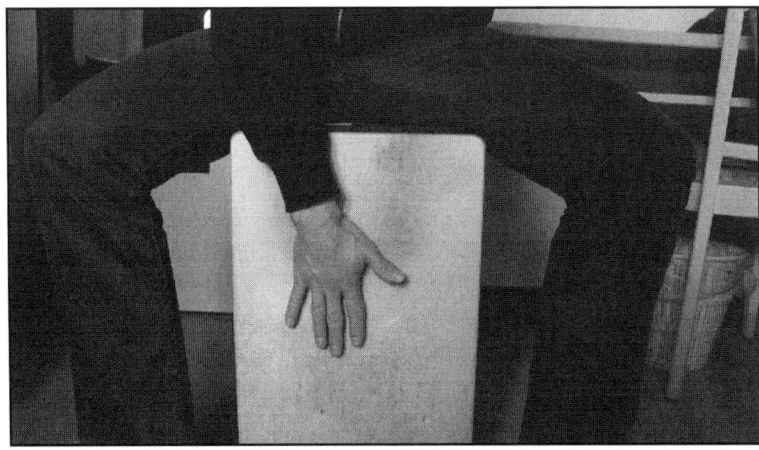

4) Depending on how tall you are, it may be easier for you to use your elbow as a pivot point or your shoulder. Experiment with these two options to find the most comfortable, relaxed way of striking the cajon.

5) Every cajon is a little different, so you'll need to find the "sweet spot" on your drum. The best bass tones can generally be found by lining the top of the cajon up with your wrist.

Sometimes the sweet spot is a little lower. As well, some people find it easier to get a preferable sound from the cajon by lightly flexing their fingers away from the drum and hitting only with the meat of their palm. This, again, if personal preference and you will have to find what works best for you.

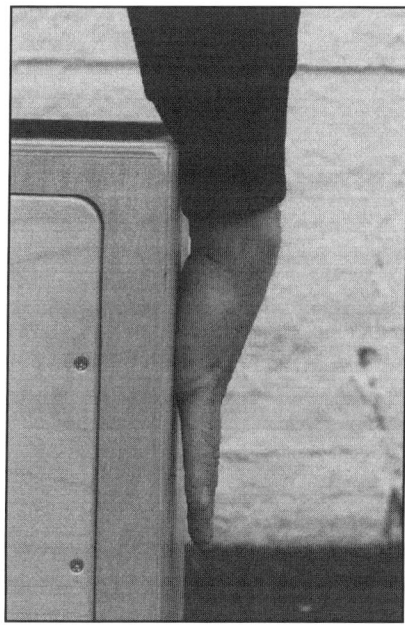

Slap Tone

1) You can either keep your fingers slightly spread as you did for the bass tone, or bring them together.

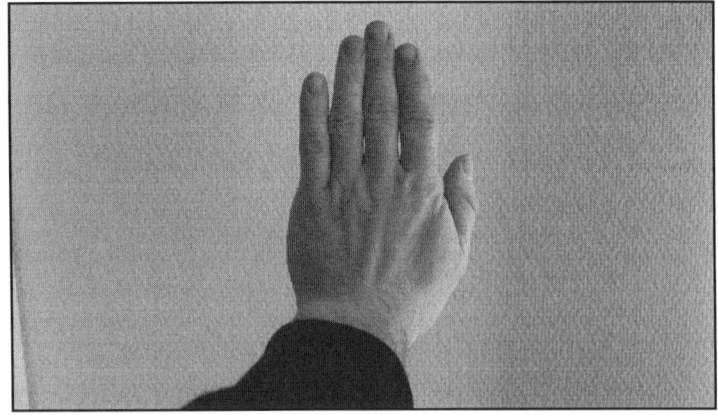

2) Place your hand so that the bottom of your fingers (where your fingers meet your hand) are at the top of the cajon.

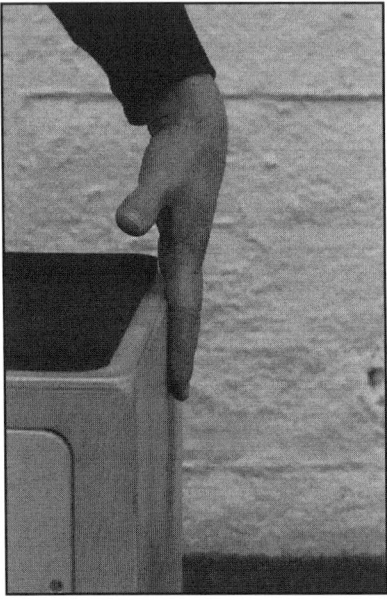

3) Using your *wrist*, strike the cajon keeping your fingers straight but relaxed. The sound you're looking to achieve is a high pitched, short yet strong sound. It's important to note that this is a wrist based motion. Your arm should be relaxed and should move as a reaction to your wrist and hand moving, but should not be the source of the power.

Basic Rhythm Fundamentals

The most important idea to grasp when we talk about rhythm is time. Musical time, much like the time we tell with clocks and watches, is a continuous activity in music. Similar to how our clocks continue to tick when we sleep, regardless of the fact that we are inactive, musical time continues to "tick" even when we are not playing, or "resting."

Rhythm, the organization of notes in time, is broken into 2 categories; notes and rests. Notes refer to when we are active or making sounds on our instrument. Resting is what is happening when we are inactive, or not making sound on our instrument. However, the important thing to remember is that when we are resting we are still COUNTING. Even when I'm not looking at my watch it's still ticking every second that goes by. We are accountable for each moment of the music we make, even when we're resting!

TEMPO

Every song has a tempo. Tempo is the heartbeat of the song. The beat at which it "pulses." In fact, the "pulse" of the song is often referred to as the tempo. We measure tempo in beats per minute, or BPM's.

If a song is a book, then the sentences of the book are the *measures* of the song, and the words of the book are the notes of the song.

MEASURE

A measure holds notes in it. We use measures so we aren't looking at a constant stream of notes, but can organize them in a format that is easier on the eyes. If every word in a book wasn't separated by periods, commas, exclamation points and questions marks it'd be much harder to read them!

1 measure

8 Measures

barline, which seperate measure (also known as bars)

Time Signature

Time signatures are a further way of organizing rhythm within our measures. Time signatures can change throughout pieces of music, but for our purposes, all examples and songs will remain in 1 time signature.

What is a time signature?

A time signature tells us how to count the song. Remember when I told you even when we're not actively playing, we're actively counting? Time signatures tell us what to count to and which notes to count.

Let's take *Happy Birthday* for example. Happy Birthday is in [3/4]. This means:
– 3 counts to the measure (we count 1, 2, 3)
– The quarter note gets the count.

What on earth is a quarter note?!

If a WHOLE measure gets divided up, it gets divided up into HALF notes (and rests), QUARTER notes (and rests) and EIGHTH notes (and rests).

Take a moment and examine the rhythm map below. You will find a handful of notes and rests used to organize rhythms.

Rhythm Map:

When trying to find what note gets the count in a time signature, we simply imagine a "1" on top of the bottom note, creating a fraction. In the case of [3/4], adding a "1" on top of the "4" gives us 1/4, or a quarter. You'll notice the quarter notes on the third line of the rhythm diagram above.

So what does all this mean, exactly?

If we were to fit the notes of Happy Birthday into measures, we would have a time signature of [3/4], and we would count quarter notes up to 3 for each measure:

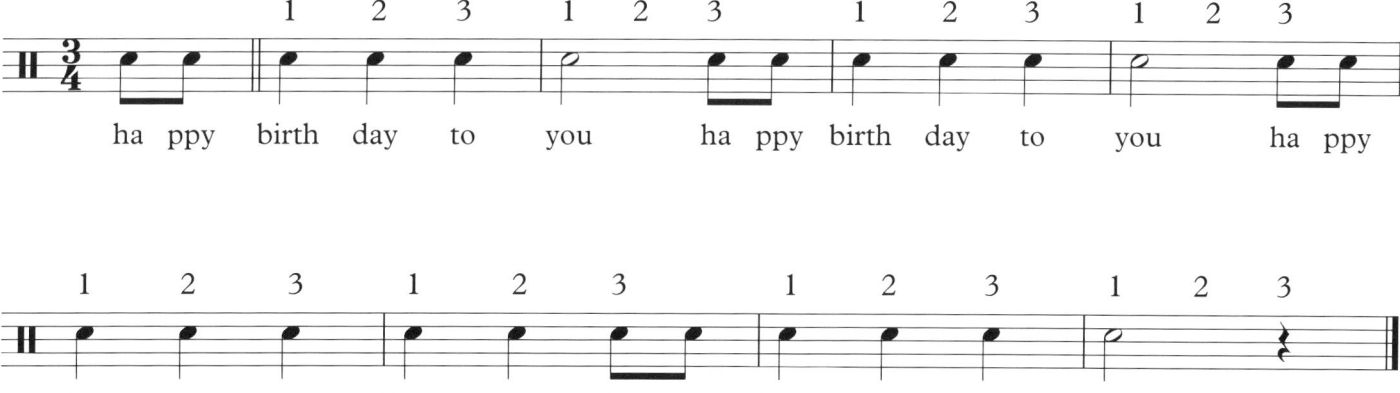

As you can see this is just the rhythm (not the melody) of Happy Birthday. Above the notes are the numbers we count out loud while playing. In this case, the we count 1, 2, 3 quarter notes per measure.

More About Counting

We've talked a little about counting quarter notes. Now we're going to speak about counting other notes.

Duration

Sometimes it's difficult as drummers and percussionists to think it in terms of duration. When we strike the cajon the sound ends almost as soon as it begins. But think about a trumpet for a moment. A trumpet player can extend the length of any note with her breath. Or a violinist who can do the same by moving his bow back and forth. A singer can simply stop and start the note with her voice. As drummers we need to remember that the idea of note length is quite important to being a great musician, even if it doesn't directly apply to our instrument!

Counting whole notes

Let's imagine that trumpet player again. To play a whole note, they must create the note on the trumpet (the same as striking the cajon) and hold that note for 4 beats. It would look and be counted like this:

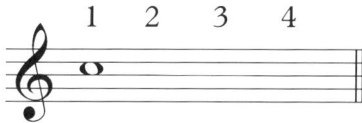

Notice how there is only one note but it lasts for 4 counts.

Now let's imagine our violinist friend has some half notes to play. The notes and proper counting would look like this:

Again, notice how the "2" and "4" don't have any attacked notes on them, but the note continues through those counts. Remember! The measure with the whole note and the measure with the half notes last for the same amount of time!

Counting Eighth Notes

In order to count eighth notes we need to add a syllable. If you look at the rhythm map above, you'll notice that 2 eighth notes take up the same amount of time as 1 quarter note. Since we count quarter notes "1, 2, 3, 4" we'll need an "in between" syllable for the extra eighth note. We count this new, extra note with the syllable "&." A whole measure of eighth notes would look and be counted like this:

If you were jamming with your friends and you wanted everyone to hit together on the 4th eighth note of the measure, you'd say "Hey guys! Let's all make a big hit on the & of 2!" This is how we communicate different points within a measure with one another. Similarly, if you wanted silence on the 5th eighth note of the measure, you'd say "I think we should rest for an eighth note on beat 3." That, by the way, would look like this:

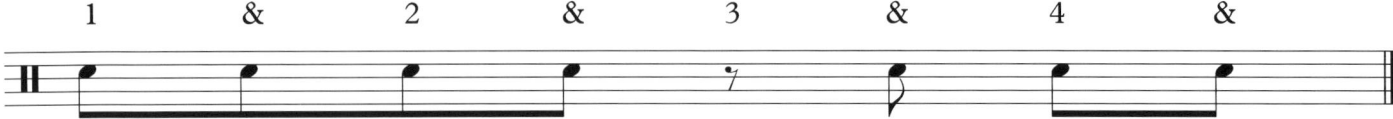

If you wanted to rest for ALL of beat 3 (not just an eighth note's worth, but the entire quarter note), it would look like this:

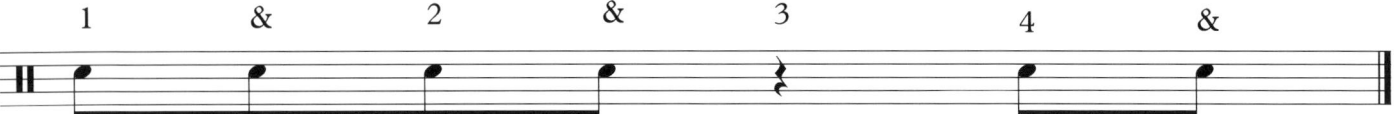

Notice how the counting changes above the staff. We shift gears into the quarter-note-mode for just 1 beat, and for that beat, we do not count using the "&" syllable.

Let's try a quick rhythm and counting exercise before we hit the cajon.

With the following examples, try clapping the rhythms and counting the appropriate syllables written above the staff. Practice these SLOW! Accuracy is far more important than speed, as it is in all aspects of music. It will never matter how fast you play something when that something is WRONG!

How to Practice

Practicing anything, be it cajon, chess, basketball, martial arts or chemistry is an art unto itself. Practicing useful, helpful exercises in a productive manner is paramount in becoming great at anything. I believe in a very simple, direct way of practicing that focuses on time, technique, sound and musicianship.

First thing's first

I believe all musicians, especially drummers and percussionists, must practice to a metronome all the time. All the time? Yes! Why, you ask? We have a responsibility to not only the listener, but to the rest of the band to keep the pulse steady. They have huge responsibilities such as key changes, pitches, chord changes, tuning, intonation and much more. The least we can do is keep the groove steady! The first step in training yourself to play with a steady beat is to practice with a metronome. All the time!

Next

Practice slowly and deliberately at first. If you are learning something new, take it slow and pay attention to every little detail. The only thing harder than learning something new is unlearning you've learned wrong! Once you begin to feel comfortable with a new idea at your slow starting tempo, you can then begin to raise the tempo by 5-10 metronome clicks. We want to be able to play confidently at all tempos.

Dynamics (volume)

The versatility we seek in tempo we should also seek in dynamics. Being able to play well at all volume levels is a key ingredient to being a great musician. Again, when learning something new, get it under your fingers at a comfortable, unchallenging tempo. Once you've got a grasp on it, see if you can play it as well as at half the volume. A quarter? Playing quietly with confidence is difficult!

Finally

For those of you not looking forward to playing exercises slowly to a metronome, this final step will make it all worth it. I'm a firm believer in playing along to recordings. It teaches you infinite amounts about music as well as your own playing. And…it's fun! Put on a recording…any recording…and play along. It doesn't matter if you don't know the beats or the song structures. Just try to keep up. Learn the beats and the song structures as you go. Pay attention to nuances the recorded musicians use in their own playing and adapt them to your own playing. Even if there isn't a cajon or drum part in the song, create one that makes sense!

OK! Let's Make Some Noise!

Now that you understand the two basic cajon strokes, let's practice them!

Notes at the bottom of the staff are the bass notes. Notes at the top of the staff are the slap notes. Practice these examples at the marked tempos with a metronome.

As you can see, the bass tone is on the lowest space of the staff ("F" if this were a treble clef) and the slap tone is higher on the staff ("C" if in treble clef).

There are many ways to practice the following musical examples. Use these 6 methods for each example. If a tempo is too fast for one particular method (left hand only, for instance), simply slow the tempo down and practice the example until you are comfortable enough to raise the tempo.

1) Right hand only
2) Left hand only
3) Right hand bass tones, left hand slap tones
4) Left hand bass tones, right hand slap tones
5) Alternating hands, starting with the right
6) Alternating hands, starting with the left

Practice all examples at the following tempos: ♩ = 50, 65, 80, 95. These are excellent starting points. If you need to go slower, that's fine. Make sure all of these tempos sound and feel good when playing each example before moving on or moving to faster tempos.

If this sounds intimidating, good! The fun part about learning a new instrument is the new world of possibilities that lay ahead. This is just the first set of many musical examples in this book, so make sure you're comfortable with them before moving on!

♩ = 50, 65, 80, 95

Sixteenth Notes

Now that you've got a grasp on whole, half, quarter and eighth notes, it's time to learn the next subdivision (to subdivide simply means to rhythmically divide notes up, as we've done with all the notes you've learned so far).

Since we know that 2 eighth notes take up the space of 1 quarter note, we also know that 4 sixteenth notes take up the same space as 1 quarter note, or 2 eighth notes. Notice the difference in look to a sixteenth note compared to an eighth note below:

Eighth Notes   Sixteenth Notes

Sixteenth note rests also look a little different. Instead of the single flag coming off the eighth note rest, the sixteenth note rest has 2 flags.

Eighth Note Rests   Sixteenth Note Rests

Remember when we added "&" to our counting when we learned about eighth notes? Well, we need to a couple more syllables in order to count sixteenth notes. Those syllables are "e" (pronounced "eee") and "ah" (pronounced "ahh" or "uhh"). "E" and "ah" are the 2nd and 4th notes in each group of 4. The 1st and 3rd notes are our original eighth notes, "1" and "&."

Counting sixteenths:

1   e   &   ah   2   e   &   ah   3   e   &   ah   4   e   &   ah

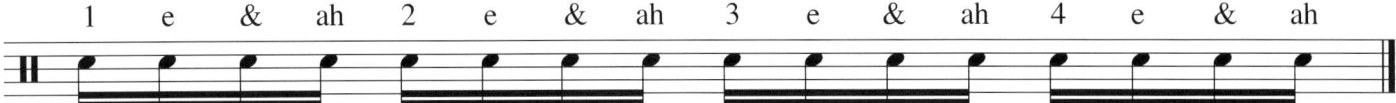

As with eighth notes, we continue to count the sixteenth note syllables even through rests:

1   e   &   ah   2   e   &   ah   3   e   &   ah   4   e   &   ah

Sometimes sixteenth notes and eighth notes get grouped together. On the cajon, there are often multiple ways of writing a certain rhythm. The following are examples of sixteenth notes grouped with eight notes, as well as examples of small musical phrases that look different but sound the same. The first two beats of each measure are one way of writing it, the last two beats are the other way.

Now that you have a basic understanding of sixteenth notes, let's play them on the cajon! Remember, take it slow. This is not race. It's music!

Track 4

12.

13.

Track 5

14.

15.

16.

17.

Track 6

18.

Track 7

19.

Ties and Dots

There are a couple more methods we use to express duration in rhythm. The first are *ties*.

If a note is tied to another note, we play the first note and hold it for the duration of the struck note, as well as the note it is tied to. So if 2 notes are tied together, we strike the instrument once and count for the duration of the 2 notes. For instance:

In this example we would strike on beats on 1 and 3. If we were playing an instrument with longer duration possibilities (violin, trumpet, timpani, voice, etc…), we would strike on 1 and hold the note through the length of beat 2, then strike again on beat 3 and hold the note through the length of beat 4.

Here are some more examples of tied rhythms:

Dots

Adding a dot to a note adds 1/2 of that note's value to itself. Let's think about the change in our pocket. If I had two quarters in my pocket, and we were able to add one of these magical, musical dots to those two quarters, they'd become 3 quarters. Since 1/2 of 50 cents is 25 cents, we add that 25 cents to our original 50 cents, giving us 75 cents or 3 quarters.

In a musical context, if we dotted a half note, it would then have the value (or length/duration) of 3 quarter notes (just like the change in our pocket above!).

Here is a musical explanation of this example:

1 half note = 2 quarter notes   If we *dot* the half note it = 3 quarter notes

Now that you understand dotted rhythms, here are some basic musical examples to play along with:
(Practice playing these rhythms both with the bass tone and slap tone.)

19

Now that you have a broad understanding of how rhythm is written and performed, let's talk about a very important fundamental of music, form.

Form

A good analogy for musical form is driving directions. In order to visit a place I've never been before, I'll need proper driving directions, right? I'll need to know where to turn right. Where to turn left. Which highway to take. Do I take it north? West? Most people think of music in one straight line; introduction, verse, chorus, verse, chorus, bridge, chorus, ending. However, if we were to write every piece of music in this linear fashion every chart (written piece of music) would be many, many pages! In music, we try to keep the amount of pages to a minimum so that the performer isn't responsible for finding his way through a book of music. Instead, especially for non-classical music, we try to keep the amount of pages below 3 or 4.

So how do we do this? Form!

Repeat Signs

Repeat signs tell us to repeat a section again. We see one repeat sign at the beginning of one measure and its companion repeat sign at the end of another measure further along in the music. It could be two measures away. It could be 200 measures. But if you see one, keep your eyes peeled for the other!

Here is what a repeat sign looks like:

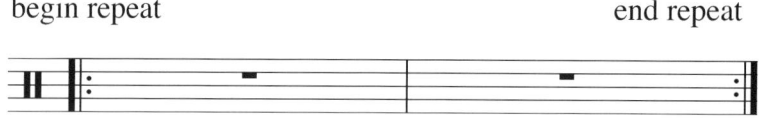

In this case, we would repeat these 2 measures one extra time, making them a total of 4 measures of rest.

Here's another example:

In this example we play the first 4 bars, repeat them once, then play the last bar, making a total of 9 bars.

Pop/Rock beats for Cajon

The following musical examples are typical beats you can play on the cajon in various Pop and Rock music settings. Some are more challenging than others. Remember! Take it slow! Use a metronome!

Often in pop and rock music, "beats" or grooves will be 2 measures in length. What this means is that the groove will take 2 measures to repeat. All of the examples so far have been 1 measure long. Try playing these 2 bar examples:

2nd Endings

Another common form direction is the use of *2nd endings*. 2nd endings allow us to write long, repeated sections with separate endings to the repeats.

In this example we would play measures 1, 2, 3, 4, then repeat. Only on the repeat, we skip the 4th measure, which is labeled with a 1st ending, and play 5th, labeled a 2nd ending.

Here is a longer example to practice. There are several repeats, incorporating 1st and 2nd endings. You can think of this as one long example, or a short piece of music. Unlike our previous examples which are 1, 2 or 4 bars in length, this is one long example.

24

Dynamics

Some would say dynamics are the most important part of music. Dynamics are simply the different volumes music is performed at. We have a series of different symbols that direct us to play at different volumes at different moments during a piece of music. A very common example of this would be playing soft in the verse and then louder in the chorus of a pop song.

Dynamic vocabulary

pianissimo - very soft

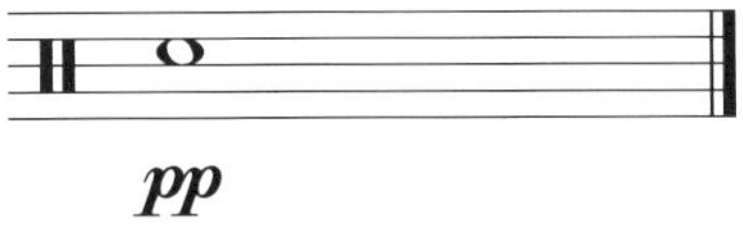

pp

piano - soft

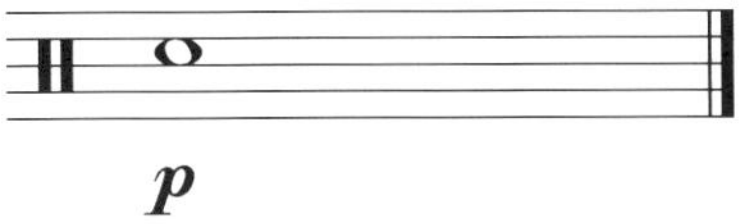

p

mezzo piano - medium soft

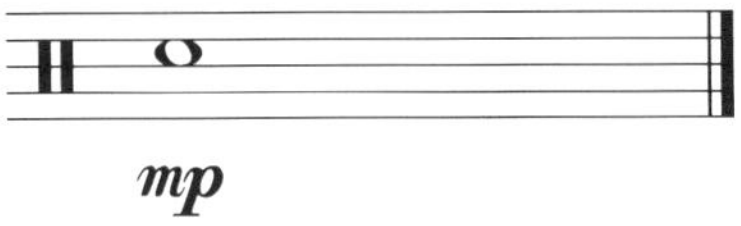

mp

mezzo forte - medium loud

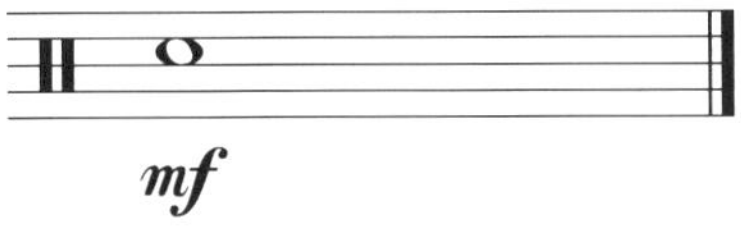

mf

forte - loud

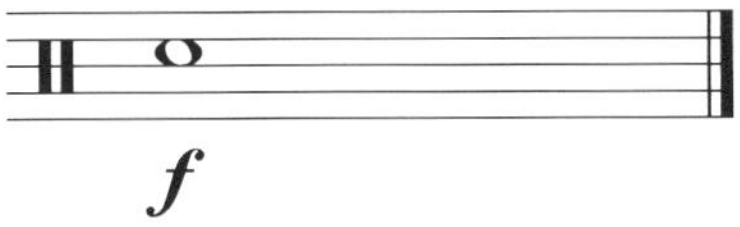

f

fortissimo - very loud

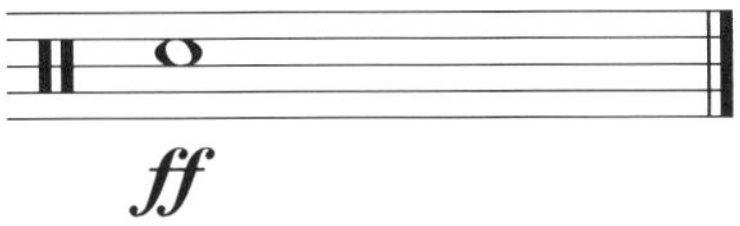

ff

Here is a short piece utilizing some of the rhythms you've seen so far along with these dynamic markings:

Ghost Notes

Ghost notes are a huge part of music - all styles, all instruments. They are subtle nuances that help shape and round out grooves.

What is a ghost note, you ask? A ghost note, put very simply, is a very quiet note among louder notes. The volume, or dynamics, of the music doesn't change, these notes just weave in and out of the music subtly.

Ghost notes are notated just like other notes, except they are in parenthesis, like so:

Brushes

Brushes are a tool adapted from the jazz drum set to cajon. The original brushes were, if you can believe it, fly swatters! There were 2 sounds drummers were looking for when they finally came up with the brush. First, they were hoping to find a softer sound than a drum stick. For styles like ballads especially, brushes became the standard musical implement. The second reason was sound length. Remember we discussed earlier in this book the idea of duration? The idea that a violinist, using their bow, could extend a single note indefinitely was an appealing idea to drummers. By lightly dragging the brush across the head of the snare (or any other) drum, the drum set player could now extend a single note to their ear's desire.

While it is perfectly acceptable to use both of these techniques on cajon, the first is the most common and useful when it comes to brushes. The pictures below will give you some ideas on how to hold brushes and how to strike them against the cajon. However, these are suggestions. I encourage you to find a grip and overall technique that is comfortable for you and suits your style!

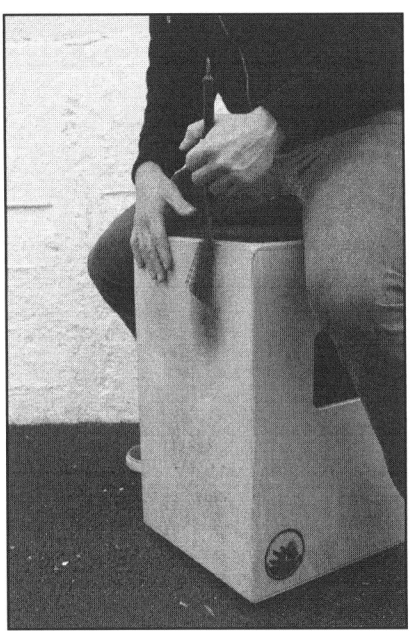 

For the following the examples, the "x" on the top of the staff represents the brush part. The bass and slap tones are in their normal places on the staff. Practice these examples both with the brush in the right hand as well as the left. You'll surely find one easier than the other but having dexterity is important as a percussionist!

Flams

In the long tradition of classical and military snare drum technique there is a vocabulary known as rudiments. Rudiments and their variations make up the basic and majority of the vocabulary for all snare drum technique and repertoire. Rudiments are divided into families and *flams* are one of those families.

Flams date back to military and marching drumming. Armies would have drummers play various rudiments, particularly flams, to signal soldiers on the battlefield (long before walkie talkies, satellite phones, etc...). In the marching community, the famous "roll off" is a fairly universal rhythm, comprised of flams and long rolls (another rudiment) to begin a marching sequence. Almost everyone is familiar with the roll off because 20th Century Films uses it to begin their theme which appears before each of their films.

How to play a flam

Flams are quite simple. They sort of sound like an intentional mistake. A single flam consists of two notes, one followed almost instantly by another. The first of the two notes, which we call a *grace note*, is quieter than the second note. The best way to set up for a flam is to position your hands like so, with one closer to the cajon than the other:

  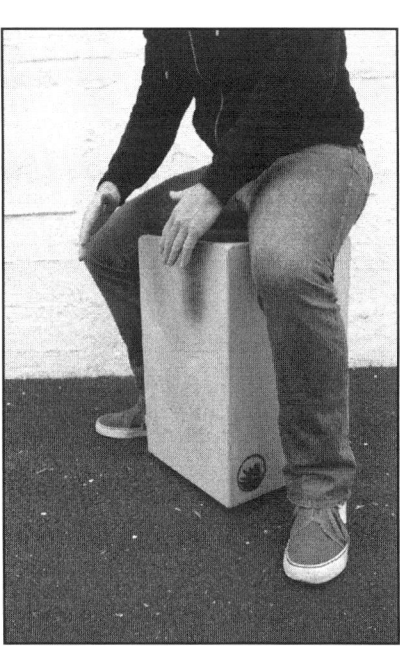

A single flam, in written form, looks like this.

grace note (quieter note which gets played just before the main note)

Here are some basic flam examples. As you can see, flams can be played with the slap tone as well as the bass tone on the cajon. Again, take these SLOW! This is a new technique that requires training both hands to move simultaneously so you may get "tongue tied" at first.

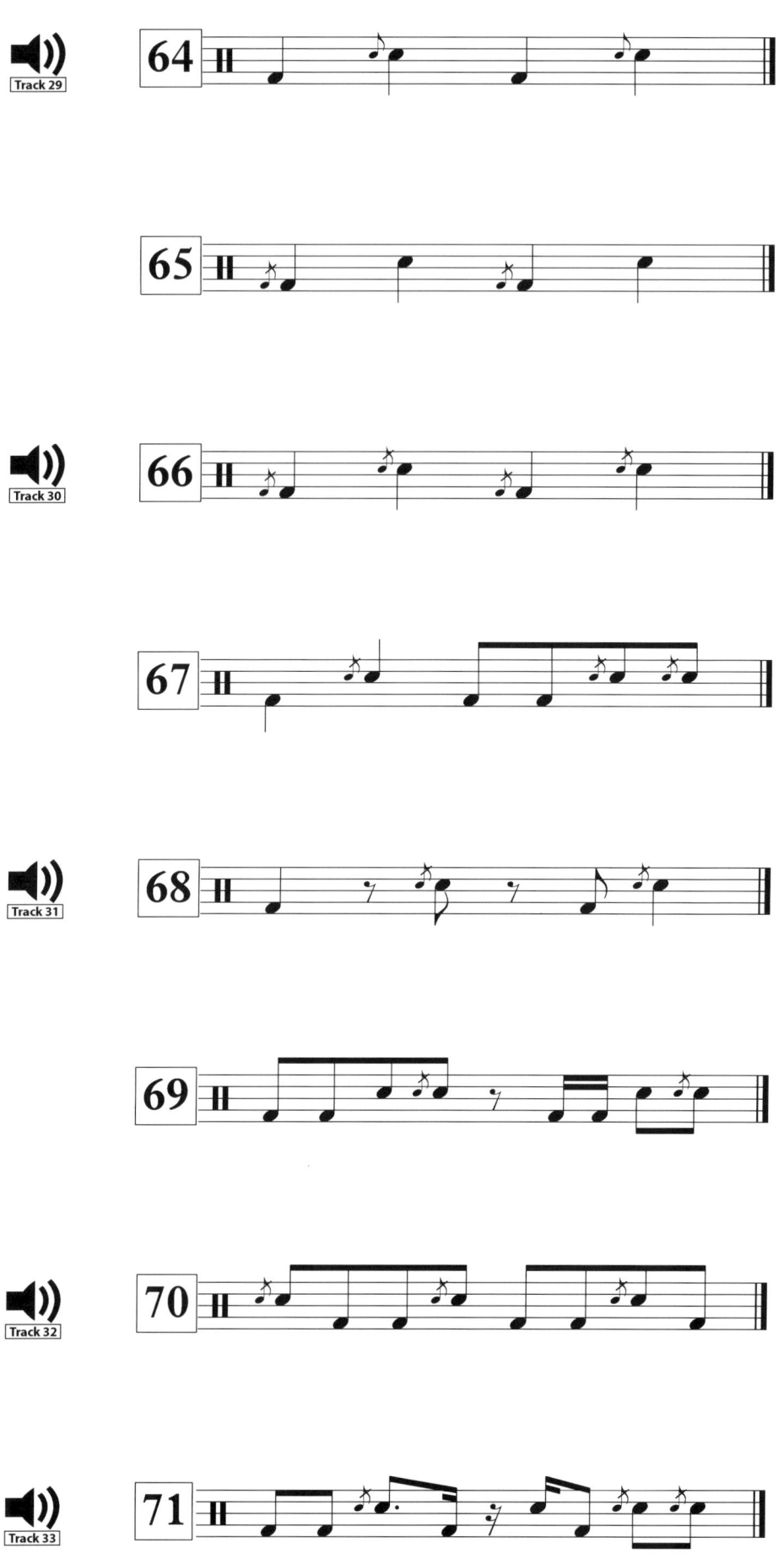

Wrapping It Up!

This book scratches the surface of the cajon. We mostly focused on the cajon in an acoustic pop/rock setting in this book. However, if you find yourself inspired to dig deeper I highly recommend delving into the traditional Spanish and Peruvian styles that the cajon is a prominent part of. Here is some recommended listening for such styles:

Paco de Lucía
Solo quiero Caminar
Cositas Buenas

Tomatito
Barrio Negro
Flamenco Es…Tomatito

Peru Negro
Sangre de un Don
Sus Raices
Zamba Malato

Nicomedes Santa Cruz
Socabon

Susana Baca
Eco De Sombras
Travesías

Now that you have a basic understanding of cajon technique and grooves it's time to start applying them! Find some friends and start jamming! One of the beautiful things about the cajon is that it is smaller and quieter than a drum set, so no excuses! If you have a friend with an acoustic guitar (and we all do!) start learning your favorite songs. The beats in this book have prepared you for everything from Doo Wop to Blues. Hard Rock to Polka. R and B to Punk. So get to it!